Published by: Experiments in Fiction

Cover photograph: Kathryn A. LeRoy

Cover Design by: Experiments in Fiction

ISBN: 978-1-7394044-4-4

Selma Martin

IN THE SHADOW OF RAINBOWS

In The Shadow of Rainbows

SELMA MARTIN

I dedicate In The Shadow of Rainbows to you, the person holding this book, the person whose presence I felt as I persevered to complete this debut poetry collection.

To you, with gratitude and admiration.

— Selma Martin

Selma's Notes:

The events that left imprints on me happened in my head and helped me to live "a reality that was felt."

As a child, I was often reprimanded for doing "bad" acts, which always started with good intentions. The reprimands were more exasperated pleas from Mother to eat my share of whatever I shared with others, who, I always felt, needed that thing more than me.

An altruistic child, a spectator who realized that when she employed her heart and mind, she was larger than the limits of her petite frame. Mind tended to point to the variegated realities of people, and Heart ordered Mind to form good realities for them.

I knew this was my agency as a thinking presence, and how I still see life unfurl.

After every reprimand, I cried real tears, not from the scolding but the teasing my siblings took upon themselves to dish out.

I'd cry from that! But always, through wet eyelashes and learning to stand under the sun just so, I marveled at the rainbows that settled on my watery eyes.

And I cried often. Hearing of people's hardships brought

out tears, literally and figuratively, I saw rainbows. Always.

This poetry collection started with me scribbling words that came, and accumulating them on paper for publishing one day. I did not start with a theme, but trusted a theme would emerge.

As you read, you'll find many poems about shadows, and so, as I filled the pages of my notebook, I also scribbled down titles about shadows. But then something happened—a happy, joyous thing, and I cried. Wouldn't you know it? The sun shone slant on me, and I recalled something I had almost forgotten about— rainbows!

From seeing rainbows on eyelashes came *In The Shadow of Rainbows*. I hope you like my debut poetry collection, and that your poem finds you.

Disclaimer: This is a work of fiction. All imagery comes from memories exclusive to the author, seen through her perspective, and translated at her discretion.

What I want my poems to do:

I want to contribute a verse in a book of poetry that celebrates people.

I want to write poems of discovery and growth rooted in awareness and presence.

I want to make the language simple while remaining true to the restrictions of rhyme and meter that make listening to poetry a pleasurable experience.

I plan to use poetry as a springboard to the sacred (even for those not looking for it).

I hope to delight my readers in lyrical prose anyone can understand.

My poetry might not change lives or even help to save anyone from their monsters. Still, I will attempt to show that redemption is possible in awareness of presence in ordinary life and, at best, offer awareness that poetry can heal if we stop for a moment to think it could help, and let poetry wash over us. I think we all have some healing to do.

Each poem in this collection satisfied me at the moment

I wrote it—it gave me a glimpse into myself at the time. That's not to say all the poems are autobiographical, they aren't, but they took me to a place where I and another soul's echo communed for a moment. I don't know whose soul but if you are that person, the poem will find you, open you up and let you feel seen.

'Are you my mother?' Each poem will ask.

I'm confident that one poem in this book will take your hand, reunite you with your echo and take you home — found and richer with you-ness for having been seen. That's what I want one poem to do for you.

I wrote them in unadorned language and let them go out to seek their own penumbra that outlines the beautiful souls of those they belong to.

In many instances the poems I labored to write didn't all turn out the way I envisaged them. Which is to say, those poems wrote themselves. Still, I'm happy, to be the conduit for you. And pleasantly satisfied that almost all the poems ended with rainbows as seen through weeping eyes.

the wind disguised from me
the cry of the river
you won't hear it either
unless you climb the bank
the poem disguised
itself from me
it hid in burrows
and places I wouldn't go looking:
inside shadows, whispers and echoes
until one day I saw rainbows on my eyelashes
— *come with me, I'll help you find your poem...*

Contents

My Shadow

My legs walk me to places
I really want to visit
but often show refusal:
Explicitly resist it.

When others zoom by past me
I turn to my dear shadow
who follows me forever
even when alleys narrow.

My legs don't seem to know me
as well as shadow does
she stops whenever I stop
or picks up speed and runs.

My anima's familiar
with my many moods and ways,
needs no code or preamble
least of all, scat song to sway:

She'd soon slide off a full moon
if legs dared walk me there
and hold my hand, enraptured
to land us fair and square.

And at bedtime, at lights out
when legs cannot be bothered
she'll be standing by the door
before the switch is triggered:

Penumbra that outlines my soul—
you are by far the best
come near me, loyal companion
lay your head upon my chest.

Confess

Don't look at me that way,
like a blank white page waiting,
imploring I succumb and confess.

You need to go away:
Can't you see dawn is breaking?
Deprived of rest, I'll face another test.

Salmon sky mixed with gray
in my mind's eye still lingers
adding, subtracting, when traps close and oppress:

Give me vigor, I pray,
or brawn to cross my fingers:
To babble what the weak would not confess.

Her Mind

Heavy with a languor
like the somnolence of noon
uncanny how she lived through the turmoil

Tears of rage and anger
stain her eyelids maroon
as she rots slow like moldering topsoil

In the bluing hour
she rouses to the thunder,
shrilling like a kettle on the boil:

The stale air that blows sour,
sunned asphalt that sickens her–
reality lands and swallows up her spoils.

Remember

It does me good to remember
how the storm swept through, bad-tempered;
cancelled events on my calendar,
grudgingly, strength I surrendered.

Locked with him in my chamber,
the hours oozed by, more tender
than ever, when we're together
it does me good to remember.

Thanks to the terrible weather
the storm will be marked forever
as igniting the dying embers
when it swept through, bad-tempered.

To never say never, ever
when dimly—see it get better—
a storm can work wonders, remember
cancels events on calendar.

Go on, pull yourself together,
love ignites a dying ember,
calls your true strength to surrender:
Blame the big moon in September.

Extra

Think of it a monetary allowance,
this extra day you're given to spend
the Giver of life does the giving,
the bounty is yours to expend.

It isn't the Giver who wills the outcome,
it's nonsense to censor the Giver so,
a liability to crowd your headspace:
The receiver may squander or sow.

Remember you promised Mother
to take your cue only from her:
Callous to lay still with torpor
awaiting another to stir.

Try hard to change what you can change,
the unchangeable, just accept
untwist from distorted logic
and better reasoning, adopt.

There's too much going on in our lifetime
bombardment of information
and stimulation of our senses,
noise all the time—distraction.

We need to shut it all down,
reboot and hear the silence,
withdraw and take a look from above—
observe with heart and soul, or else!

On this day given you by the Giver
put the squanderer to rest
call forth the Sower of hope
and from within, bring out your best.

Surrender

How wrong to invent excuses,
blue moments in the present lie
strive not to weigh the prominence
of displeasure and pleasure alike:

Get subsumed, merge with the instant
not in days past nor future
take your place in the brief present
court blue moments as they arise.

They happen when least expected,
in short times of love or terror,
perceived only in memory
to reside gently in the mind.

Then, like pearls, come down from heaven,
those junctures gift you a recall:
seize each ephemeral instance
court the blue moment, surrender.

August Trio

August
you brought hope in—
a glamour all your own
summer fairies are departing
shift change

Jealous
moonbeams react
with phantasmal cold stares
Sun is gentle in September
enchant

in turn
Ms. Bumblebee
appears at my window
next, Longlegs and Moth scuttle near
—so long.

Kindled Echoes

To the sway of the palm trees
I pause in recollection.
The laps of the cool breeze
start my introspection:

Synopsis of the past
imprinted on my mind
pixelated light, intact,
too good to leave behind.

The mist parted at last,
as did youth's bitterness
and, though the blush sank fast,
remains your soft caress.

My heart shares residence
with one other: that's you,
one key unlocks the bliss
to love like this anew.

Richest are the echoes
of whispers at half-light
which make for good bedfellows
that in the dark, ignite.

The House

In two decades of decadent living,
I'd banished all remembrances of the past,
but the house that I ran from came ghosting
nudging me to revisit one last time.

Jack Daniel's, Thaddeus IV, and I hit the road with trep-
idation,
our trio will make do the best we can.
Surprisingly, my brain's GPS knows the way precisely:
by noon, we stand before the squalid house.

I take a swig to boost me up and numb my senses,
no need to get worked up over a childhood that's buried
and gone,
but then Thaddeus IV's growling comes with cryptic ur-
gency
that sends him in a wild dash to the back of the house.

I hug Jack like a shield to protect my galloping heartbeat
and barrel us in the direction of the barking dog
but my foot catches, sends Jack rolling and me floundering
until crying and full of sulk, I spit out the hurt from
chicken-shit dirt.

Give Back

perfect specimens
of imperfection
you and I
cocoons in the universe
surviving
thriving
reproducing
loving
living
nurtured under the illimitable
distant sun, fulfilling stories
among starlight
may we soon rise
to the role
we cannot leave
to chance

Let Go

Light illuminates
all who wander
in darkness and delusion,
transports them to
a blissful dawn:
Let go
and revel in
the luminous
afterglow
albeit the godforsaken
bump along the road.

When Death Comes

When death comes
I don't want to look back
lovelorn, empty, frightened
—Oh, no!
When death comes
I want to be led into eternity
curious, full of joy
knowing the world I leave
is better for the love I gave.

Instinct

A butterfly in the classroom
pregnant, stiff from sleep
flips around the closet broom,
grateful broom guarded her kip.

She pats her bump, dusts off her wings,
rises to the ceiling,
and just like that, to the light, she swims
instinct prompts her milkweed landing.

You Know Her

Like clockwork, she steals over the horizon
and for a moment, hides between the blinds,
slowly she sluices me with her aura,
and on my eyelashes, perches twined.

One dawn, I met her in the forest
bright-eyed, beaming at the break of day
but then she tended to the flowers
and then she dazzled me with her rays.

Since then, she's waited for me outside tunnels
and each time, she's brought that otherworldly scent
that lifts me up and affirms I'm in good hands
and reminds me to remain in the present.

One rainy summer, she made me the happiest
when she let me peek inside the lining of her coat:
a rainbow of blinding light as I'd never seen
one more indulgence that wins my vote.

She's the one who will slide off a full moon
to land gently at your feet like a spark
and retire so you can see stars or fireflies
so you're never afraid of the dark.

And at bedtime, when the night is deepest,
and the stars compete to be your star bright
you'll still smell her under the lampshade—
like a bright idea you can use at first light—

when like clockwork, she'll steal over the horizon
to sluice you with her zest and charm, renewed
and on your eyelashes perch, coquettish
to help you seize another day with gratitude.

Enough

Enough! Enough griping over
what it'll take for us to "make it."
All this not talking to strangers,
this building of fences, this not
trusting the very air that blows.
What's the use of "making it" if
I must go the distance alone?
You grieve over the same, too,
don't you? I know you want to
talk to strangers, above all,
those wearing worn-out shoes and
threadbare clothes, the color of
sunsets— and skin the tinge of
home-baked bread, and wise eyes that
have witnessed things your pampered,
plastic life could never grasp.
You must talk to them! Forget
tall fences. You want to feel
the sun on your face, the touch
of the wind, the melody of their
spoken language, of which only the
smile you understand. Together we
can create a life that ebbs and flows
like the tide that never competes or
berates the other for its ways. Or thinks
the other odd. The cadence of our pulsing

heartbeats, the vibrant yellowness of our
favorite spring flowers, and sharing of our
stories will help us make it. Together.
Enough, I say! Draw near and let me hug you.

That Sea

When I come to extinguish the dread drowning me
and you distract me with palm trees swaying to your rage
and your fine brown sand clings to me,
I forget the worry, I come to air.

Then you dwarf me with your magnificence:
I smile, so fond of your temerity.
But you gobble up my words the moment they're spoken
and cunningly, you bid me close to wet my skirt.

Speak louder, you demand—you cannot hear me.
And so, hoarsened, I exhort the surging storm.
Louder! you can't apprehend my words—
if briefly, you'd calm your growling, you'd hear fine.

Strangely, the exertion relieves all pressure, and
I return home lucid for spewing my disquiet so.
There are no goodbyes, only cosmic see-you-later.
My sea, you invigorate me when I'm drowning.

Golden Durability

Patched up here and there with gold alloy to
preserve malleability, Mom's bracelet keeps the mark-
ers.

She wore that bracelet everywhere, and I
cannot remember a time when it didn't dangle on her
wrist.

To the chagrin of the others, who wished
it melted and reformed, I inherited the artifact.

What kind of abrupt movement cut through the
heavy-duty set hinges to become unchained from its
source?

If gold is so precious, why does it break?
And what makes one want to reform it to erase the mark-
ers?

I inhale the gold band and slide my hand
in to sense what Mom suffered. I pretend it's her wrist
I kiss.

There Is No Crime*

Unhindered by shadows that Daylight brings,
Night moves in slow, measured steps
as if cradling a sleeping infant.
A tailwind fanning warmly through trees
glides Night along, glowing, alert but shadowless.

Squirrels that had scurried in the sun paused
and preened in verdant trees,
and sparrows that had fluttered and perched to sing
in bird words that there was no crime,
now rest in the folds of Night's long robe.

There was no crime!

There was no crime,
for when the watchman descends,
all boundaries disappear:
outlines of houses and buildings fade.
Mountains and forests, sun-drenched
and clothed in umbra,
now surrender, and Earth reverts to her ancient shape
of one whole—
cradling all
in a tender embrace.

By and by, the night watchman is the first to notice
when Dawn stirs.
With pride, Night lets the infant go and
awakens the squirrels and sparrows,
sending them out to revive
all that had slumbered.
And it's only then that Night exhales,
relieved for the completion of his role.

And, having kept his pledge
of ensuring there was no crime
Night entrusts Daylight with the task
of guarding the oath.
And so, Night turns from the light,
whispering assuredly,
there is no crime; there is no crime.
And, like a fat bird waddling
follows his lengthened shadow
and trudges into a deep cave to sleep.

*The title of this poem is taken from *Mrs Dalloway*
by Virginia Woolf

Could It Be?

Could it be that my renegade
heart wasn't paying attention?
Could it be,
Could it be?

Just when I thought
the warm days would never cease
days of sitting, tracing clouds—
Clouds that had somewhere else to be.

Days of cat naps and dreamy languor
of prancing bare-legged,
running into sprinklers,
of looking for the shade
as the day
oozed by,
hour after hour;

Days too bright,
too humid,
that the cottage-trees' mosses,
in their short haircuts,
tossed encouragement at the Impatiens
that had stopped smiling.

Could it be that my renegade
heart wasn't paying attention?

Just when I thought
the warm days would never cease
one insect-eaten leaf slowly separates
and drops from the tree

that leaf,
the first one to notice
the thermostat drop
the day's length shorten;
intelligently called forth its strength
to activate the abscission process.

Just when I thought
the season would never cease,
a salacious wind comes and lifts my skirt.
I shiver, embarrassed,
and turn just in time to see the leaf levitate
and coax another leaf to play.

Could it be that this
idea of letting go is a
seed planted within us?

Could it be that, like in nature,
we are to call forth strength
to activate the abscission process—
To let go to grow?

It could be.
It could be.

Compass

Dad chose the safest landscapes,
scoured the sanest grounds,
set out in secure adventures,
cloaked his son in warmth, profound.

Dad let him scout and push boundaries
after noticing his gentle touch,
shadowed him with loving eyes,
helped him build bridges, robust.

But one day, years older,
Dad found the world in arrears:
a discord of stubborn viewpoints
and Dad's concern brought fears.

The world we've made,
is the world we failed, Dad worried,
a father can't afford to stay hushed
he gained strength, and prayers unloaded:

I want you to be men of good hearts
braver than me, your cares to the wind
to never lose your gentle touch—
let your moral compass be your tailwind.

To never do harm to yourselves or others
to never pass judgment on others' misgivings
be men of beliefs, open to learning
guided by faith and the miracle of living.

Holding firm to great hope in his old heart
confident was he in all sons' moral scope
and no youngster anywhere went astray
as for all sons, there exists hope.

I Block The Sun

The sun elongates my shadow
and the butterflies raise their guard
and flit off until my shadow and I pass.

The koi in the stream rise to the
top when I lean over to look,
and open their mouths as if we were breadcrumbs.

Odd: how could they feel my presence?
—as if life was all about me—
when with my impulsiveness, I blocked the sun.

Later, I see a doe nibbling
in the woods. Afraid to alarm
her, I halt—willing my shadow not vex her.

From afar, I see the sun-splashed
across her neck, pinking her ears;
near blinded, I blink as it reflects on me.

I open my mouth and smoke the
mirrored light in. I picture a
sun ray reaching the moon and spilling on me.

Carousel

Revolving slowly, comes the carousel
with a cache of half-forgotten memories
lands me on broad sand beach, unease does quell
till ebb and flow reveals polarities

Now levitate the sepia photos
in ever-spinning reels of love, genteel:
whirling, churning me in clouds, nebulous,
and prompt me to climb on, and next to feel

The purple light of morning steals through curtains
I feel your arm laid heavy on my chest
a grateful smile curls, no more uncertain—
glad to have you by my side—I'm blessed

In dreams, the carousel comes in to teach
succumb, recovery is within reach.

Intention

It's a worthy cause, so start the hunt
for a calm place to inhabit,
it merits more than trends to uphold
untethered from modish habits.

But who, pray tell, marooned us here,
like beached whales needing assistance?
How to find the point of return,
wake to the sacred solutions?

Take heed of the words of elders
whose hardships built strength for tomorrow,
their toil can inform your todays
and their load, lighten your sorrows.

Don't be seduced by "you can't lose,"
gains do not come from wins alone;
balance holding on, letting go,
apologies, kudos unsung—

the calmest place to inhabit,
anchors safely inside of you
but look for it with intention,
confident that you will find it.

Failure

The world is wrecked, we finally admit,
has come to a freeze, run its full course
and unwittingly drained us of life-force.

Well, with lies about outer shells
that are supposed to look sexy
until everyone suffers, grave apoplexy.

We've sniped at each other's foibles
when one brother tumbled, added fuel
and preached from doctrines that are cruel.

Grown numb to pureness and empathy;
grown cold, mean, capricious, and blithe
—disregarding the others' limits.

Made holy the damn easy button,
clasped at gadgets and mind-changing balms
that bring instant ease, figments of calm.

Imbibed the open-at-all-hours mindset
that proclaimed sleep as outmoded—
how in the world could rest be outdated?

Fit in to a world that grumbles much,
stockpiles it all; witty raconteurs
that stand in stages of heights of grandeur.

That old world's broken, upended,
it has completely derailed us;
but have trust, the upgrade will unveil us.

But only if we change to the new angle
of a better truth—equity leads to equality,
one story of love and camaraderie.

What if, in two hours, the upgrade would start?
Would you be ready to transcend?
You will be if you go beyond with pure intent.

Nature's Tender Doings

The green outside is winking at me;
it arose merely moments ago,

like a well-rested child rising from sleep,
its radiance is dewy with stardust.

It twinkles my way, coos me to play
in one more unplanned day of wanderlust.

The air is still cool, and each blade of grass—
its hairs stiff from gazing at the night sky,

reflects now the sun, invites me to pause
and to join in like the morning's lightness.

I gaze for a while; my smooth hair stands tall
stiff in the pristine freshness of daybreak.

My cheeks, like a child's, are puffed and still warm
remind me I'm not just a spectator.

Just then, the bluebells start their morning chant,
and I, barefoot, must sprint out to join them.

Poetry

I came out to write a nature poem
out here by the silent trees
cloaked in deep concentration
to prove my mind's prowess.

Oh, if only the bees would stop buzzing
and the squirrels would hurry with their tasks!
Ah, if the birds would cease chirping
and grant me peace and quiet at last.

I came out to write a nature poem
about squirrels, birds, trees, and me,
but I've been dazed with distractions—
think I'll go for a nature walk to see.

As I steal close to the duck pond,
I find them enraptured in lessons today,
so I sit down to write my nature poem
and hope that they don't interrupt me.

But an owl hoots at me from a distance,
and the cicadas start to sing,
butterflies pirouette on my shoulders,
Geez, can't a poet do anything?

I put aside pen and paper
And drift to the red hibiscus
Find a *zunzuncito** in midair frisk
diving and fluttering its tail feathers

And I think to myself,
I came out to write a nature poem,
but of poetry writing, I learned this
in attempting to write, I must fuse with it,
for in nature, the poet exists.

zunzuncito—bee hummingbird.

For Farah

Into the nothingness of noise
I strain to voice my cares with you,
into the scornful sea that drowns
my dreams and cares, to you, unknowns.

Yet still, I labor night and morn
to reach the one without a smile.
We're under the same sky and moon
and for you my arms are open wide.

Last night you popped into my dreams
barely a shadow with shoulders stooped
and when your shadow vanished in the crowd
the spot was wet where you had stood.

You are the consumer of your woes*
that rise and linger like a storm-cloud
you know I'm here but in your stifled throes
you choose to scorn and imitate the proud.

I know you haven't smiled in ages
you find your queen bed vexing when you lie.
Bah humbug! My old, disgruntled friend,
the clock ticks and you're drowning in your guise.

*consumer of your woes: the "self-consumer of [his]
woes"— from the poem 'I Am!' by John Clare

Replete

Full of sulk, she loathes the boredom
all alone in her village home.
A bird chirps, and a baby coos:
Sun-kissed strawberries, grilled-cheese blues.

She props the baby in the pram
beside them walks the newest lamb
they sit under the poplar tree,
the babe, the lamb, a book, and she

And the daylight isn't long enough
but her life is plentiful, though tough
and the blazing orange yonder
blesses her with awe and wonder

Wrapped in visions which come in dreaming
she glides through that bluing evening.
A lank, tan cat slinks languidly,
she walks behind it happily.

Angel August

In the depths of my convalescing dungeon,
with a nurse who spoke non-stop in a foreign tongue,
I lost claim to my God-given faculties,
lost track for a while of the calendar days

Thank God, Nurse insisted on muscle strengthening
that he managed alone while I slept
then he'd lift me, transport me outdoors,
and plant me there like a tender rose.

He made sure the cushions supported my limpness
and that my bare feet on the earthen ground lay
then he'd run off next door for respite and peace
leaving me to the buzz of bumblebees.

One fine day, I recognized the smell of summer,
the languid air of the somnolent noon,
so I rose and walked away from the wheelchair
hands outstretched, to the hollyhocks there.

Months later, I learned this was a daily routine
in his three months of tending me with care
but that fateful August day that the hollyhocks called
was the first I'd remember after nothing at all.

I owe my recovery to my carer,
and the grace that surrounds me day by day,
and to blue skies, flowers, butterflies, and bees
and to August—the aptest name for my angel
who didn't live to see the Fall.

Something's Broken

That scraping, maddening sound,
that creaking and groaning I hear–
like iron on iron
that rises with the wind
and is followed by the loud bark
of a neighbor's dog
  if that dog hears it,
  everyone in this sleepy coastal town does

But what is it?

Anything could make such a mad sound,
the swinging of a gate,
halyards slapping on the mast of sailboats,
metal dragging on cement
mattress springs,
faulty wheels on a pram,
whale calls, or
marriage-vows renounced

The dogs are anxious tonight
yes, halyards clang; mine are frapped tight.
  Something scrapes that shouldn't scrape
  something's stuck that shouldn't be
  something promised to last ends
– something's broken

That moaning and rasping strains
heavy on the wind tonight.
Do you hear it too?

Poseidon's Lure

Exhaustion is the anchor
that tonight hangs 'round my neck
bowls me over and roils me
makes of me a ragdoll wreck

the anchor downward pulls me
to a space 'tween this and that
where fear and worry strand me,
makes me feel at home at last

can't fight the powers that be
for the *Merak* of slumber
the shy soul that houses me
drops to depths unencumbered

Ebb and Flow

no
matter
how much we
try to prolong
the day to make it
last longer, eventide
arrives, bearing nuances
of untrammeled virtues, in tones
of splendidly tinged life lessons that
lend wisdom to the most facetious
until we come to see our uniqueness,
not sabotaging the ebb and flow
that gets us closer to the sky
where we embrace our essence
face to face reflected
in our human-ness
to help us thrive
in the waltz
of each
hour

Shadows

The world's held together by shadows
that flit around and lurk behind the light:
come forth, come forth, my faithful shadow
the sun is far away, the moon hides,
come hither now while darkness abides.
One shadow races past the others
and, in a grip of fury, grabs my hand
twirls me around, that ruffian shadow
from behind a cloud, springs forth the moon
peace holds court in the hush of its light
and I feel I've had too much champagne.

Listen

There is a voice I cannot silence,
I must obey and write it down,
I never asked for company this early
I wanted to write about fruit trees and bees
and butterflies dipping into flowers first
and learn to add a melody to the page

but that voice keeps interfering,
insisting I listen. But when I do
I hear husky groans and sobbing
of a grown man who wants me
to interject for him instead—
something about a transgression.

I see the smoke from his pipe rise
and slither out the window.
I do not seem to understand:
Are you the writer, old man, or am I?
Am I the river, or are you?

Day After Shining Day

She returns daily at 4:40 sharp.
You'd suppose she holds a watch in her hand.
We lock eyes like yesterday, heads slant,
but she smirks as if I were the prowler.
Lady squirrel on my fence, Madam,
yours is a magnanimous commission
I'm running low on toilet paper,
stores on Saturdays close at 6 pm
I best get on with my great mission
carry on, carry on, little lady
before summer's bounty closes in on you.

Circle of Earth

The white picket fence outside your window
is the norm you take life to represent
in your suburb, the mother and father
are as normal as the golden ladder
in level seven of the circle of heaven.

All seeped in Jupiter's justice, that ladder,
an arc that lives in the imagination,
for deeper introspection to advance you
and help you become a useful conveyor;
in the ordinary of ordinaries, your mind, enliven.

Oh! That to Me

Oh! That to me, a pair of wings were given,
I'd hover me above the sea I love
abide inside that faithful hour and stand awhile.
My ears would perk as Merfolks sound bassoons,
Then I'd will my heart to dive beneath the waves—
primordial home, where fury there is none.

Oh! That to me, a pair of wings were given
like a child, I'd glide with the tide, dwell in the swell
then galumph all the way to heaven
to lay my head on a soft cloud
and listen to stories from my ancestral clan
to preserve forever vaulted, like the sea in gray.

Bedeviled

I awake with a knot in my neck
the dreams that came retreat to the deck
but the noxious night dragged on too long
my suspect head perceives something wrong
a tangle of clothes muddles the floor
shattered glass blocks a dash to the door
a bird knotted in a sticky mess
provokes panic and swells my duress
the dream ends with an urgent message—
That Pandora, never a box possessed!

Songs of September

Aye, the transitory heat
of the unwelcome
fly-by-nighter that is August,
damaged my night of sleep again
nary a three-wattled bellbird whistled
hardly a swallow twittered near or far
anywhere in the sky

Aye, where are they—
the songs of September?
As we cross the meridian into Fall?
A winnowing wind disturbs the grass,
my hair soft-lifts
and ghost sandflies fidget and slide off
my legs and scuttle away like crabs
while a kite swoops for a fish.

Insomnia

A Persian cat I become every night
when I slide next to him in bed,
but it matters not how silent or smooth,
my efforts are for naught.
What time is it?, he asks, still full of sleep,
he always needs to know what time it is.
'3:04' says the clock on the stand;
just past midnight, I lie again
and smile at his drool
and the whistle of his snore
as, like a cat, I slide in
to stare at the shadows that dance
and I wait for sleep to claim me—
so it goes, so it goes, and so it goes.*

*This line is inspired by Kurt Vonnegut's *Slaughter-house-Five*

Krakow Nights

I like best the autumn days
when the windows fog over with steam
and the house delights in smells
of anise, cinnamon, and cumin.

When the boys return home from school
lugging bags that deform their small bodies
over starving stomachs that expand
with every footstep they take through the door.

The man-sized bags slide off their shoulders
and the excitement in their voices
bounces off whitewashed kitchen walls,
then soon after, we hear the car stop.

And we see feet walk through the same door,
dragging a face that lights up the room.
Then as I turn the chops, I say,
"three minutes guys, three more minutes,"

And I sprinkle a coat of Krakow Nights
and Dill Weed—both, and as I toss the chops
I turn to him, smiling, and he smiles back
Krakow Night!—I love the autumn too.

No Sugar

Don't knock on my door when you run out of sugar:
I have no sugar to spare.
But knock hard your knuckles if you run out of garlic,
sun-seeped in hours of care.
Or better yet, knock if you bring something
sizzling from the oven—made with your hands
I'll invite you to come in, serve it on *Talavera*,
and if you like, I'll teach you to dice *Jalapeños*
we'll become deserving neighbors, and in time,
good friends turned cousins— you will see!

Then I'll share with you my homemade paste of *tama-rindo*
that improves digestion and helps rid you
of parasites that crave sugar
unless you think me too plebeian for growing garlic
on my south-facing porch.
Then I won't invite you to taste my *Aguas Frescas*—
hibisco and *horchata*
that I serve in glass tumblers passed down from *Abuelita*
until then, do not come knocking for sugar.

*Jalapeños, tamarindo: spicy peppers and Spanish
word for tamarind.
Abuelita: grandmother
Aguas Frescas, hibisco and *horchata* are drinks.
Talavera: Lovely Mexican pottery

Song for Kenji

Erotic is his link to nature
as he walks the meadow,
the hill and the woods

a mere half day to get it all in
gentle his light footsteps
rhythmical, his stride

deeper his exertion, climbing higher
a kite circles
and so he tips his hat,

tickseed—he calls them silent kisses—
cling to his clothes, fusing
him with the landscape even more

he gazes up at the kite again
the earth grates at his feet
pleased, he lets escape a deep exhale

head high, long lunges—he remembers
a pale watercolor
absorbs miasma

and floats him over acacia trees,
rice fields, junipers and
cryptomeria

the kite's wind augments his levitation
he grips his hat
blue phosphorescence

a subdued luster flickers *come close*
Kenji, tickseed, and hat
tour the Milky Way

the sky is still blue when his feet alight
on clover and Kenji Miyazawa trots home
in time for supper.

Kenji Miyasawa: (1896-1933) "A famous Japanese poet, who drew on nature in a way no other modern Japanese author had before him." Inspiration for this poem of Kenji Miyasawa arose from the commentary on Kenji Miyazawa's poems, translated by Roger Pulvers' poetry collection, *Strong In The Rain—Selected Poems*. Pulvers described Kenji as he came to know him through talks with the poet's relatives.

Little Vessel

In the near reeds, the little vessel floated
like a little boat slack-towed astern.
The sea, contrite and docile
its head hung low, is dressed in black.
She let the team pull from her skirts,
the lifeless vessel—a small little thing—
but she knows not; there is no telling
if it's of the two-year-old little boy
gone missing from his home
a whole fifteen days ago.

Fifteen days ago, the marsh lilies were
resplendent—
pale purple, thriving in torrents of rainfall
searching canals, rice fields, and shrubbery
the search party scoured the land—
and then today, in the nearby marshes,
there are no more lilies
only reeds and a little vessel
carried astern by the tide
that housed the soul of a child.

The day my two-year-old
little boy went missing
the sea was gray and angry-boiling,
the fish swam high with the tumbling waves
and the seagulls were obnoxious and loud.
But my son lay at the police station
alive and whole and missing no more.
I thanked my God hard, and the daffodils
that designed this happy ending for my home.
But thenceforth, in the marshes of my soul
has dwelled a black river guzzling a monsoon
and now, at every summer's end will loom the vision
of a little vessel floating by the reeds.

I Almost Died

I almost died of exuberance
snorkeling around the unspoiled
coral reef
when, in the dull hum of silence
a green sea turtle,
in her place in this world
passed under me,
oblivious

and next, the blue tang—
the regal tang,
escorting, coaching,
tour-guiding a parade of
butterflyfish
distracted me from my keeping,
throwing me off guard:
perplexed and unready;
twirled me in a new direction.

By and by, my guide's shadow
hovered over me—
a dark cloud
that kept coming closer and closer
giving exaggerated signals
to hasten

head above water, the sound of the
squawking birds and the sea wind
swoosh in, magnified.

I bob in the water to replay the sound
I bob in the water to tease rainbows
stuck to my eyelashes and over and over,
I almost die of exuberance.

Death

Last night, past the twilight hour
I lay down in the hammock
to think—think about death,
but in my snooze-sharpened penchant
sleep trapped me, and I surrendered

I saw islands of summer lilies
basking in a cyclone of light
I had to squint through my lashes
as, fluttering in and out of pale shadows,
angels danced in surly rapture.

One took my hand—I was one with them,
then someone shouted out with joy—
stunned, I realized that the shouter was me!
I was alive, awake, and present

When I rose from the hammock, I thought
'perhaps there's no darkness in death
maybe death is about light
the kind of light that wraps around you
and forms imprints that fly on dragonfly wings—
ephemeral recalls, dormant but not forgotten.'

South-Southwest

What about the little stars,
Daughter says,
Mom turns to look—
nothing there!
Nothing but pebbles
scattered in the moonlight.
Mothers don't understand,
the little girl says.

Later, tidying the discards
of the child
Mom feels her 8-year-old hand
reach for a net
fragrant with bubble gum.

"Just to the clearing,"
she hears her mother say.
one more step, and
she's past the clearing
racing clouds
swooshing this way and that
— gasp! Stars lay dazed,
smelling of fruit gum--
laughing stars
in her net!

Mighty her wrist that flings them
before her mother finds out
then that night
her net lies weeping
baffled but still aglow
she creeps to it and
the stars sprint to her bed.

The wind, the thief of Mom's silence
comes riding a quiet surf—
she hears it slide through the
shadows of the trees in the yard
then on the wind crystals on the porch
the lilac fog, come like
a whiplash of memory
arisen from tides lain
south-southwest in her soul parts,
Mom warms and
brims over.

A river of quiet enters,
Mom moves to the window
and sees them— her daughter's
shiny barnacle-studded sea stars
strewn in plain sight of the moon.
Mom hears someone laughing—
she's laughing!
and suffers a secret
thrill that her mother never
ever understood.
Or did she?

Never Will I Not Remember

All my life, as far back as I remember
rain falls from clouds in torrents from the sky
with my own eyes, I've seen this happen
never in a trice questioning how or why

after the rain, puddles get a whopping celebration
from children splashing and laughing, barefoot
except for when it's Sunday and mothers with lower
lips
swollen with bitterness, dress children
in church clothes, frilly socks, and glossy shoes.

But all my life, as far back as I remember,
I've wondered why the puddle lingers for so long:
don't it know! children dislike leather shoes
itchy clothes, and pouty mothers
and that Sunday rain, only temptation brings.

Then one day, home sick with the mumps,
no clouds overhead but for one puddle
looking sickly, like me, under the blue sky
I saw it cower and go dry and directly,
buckets of rain came falling from the sky:

Rain comes from the ground, not clouds.
All my life, never will I not remember.

To Be A Flower

roaming lonesome through the meadow one day
the wind planted a wild idea in my head

oh! to be a flower in such meadow
pish! to be visited by a human— not a bee

a human lends no worth to a flower
no value comparable to the open field

like exists in the selfless hearts of bees
yet flowers, vulnerable all day in the meadows

must resign to such meddlesome visits
when humans come to graze, full of hallelujah

and take leave with arm-loads of wildflowers
Gadzooks! Forgetting their hallelujahs

and for another minute, revel in their capture
to soon return to their accustomed quirks

First Win

Hopeful one morn
would bring them much closer
She, barely eight
and he forty-three
Dawn after dawn
they braved nightly slumber
Tasting 'n writing,
chewing words, hungry.

The dim of the lamp
paled with new morning light
Sent them upstairs
to bowls of warm porridge
Then holding hands
to streets wet with sunlight
She to midge class went,
he to seek courage.

Until one dawn
at the turn of the lights
they reached the end
—one book defeated!
She grinned ear to ear,
and soared like a kite
Heil to her Pa,
who Ma called pigheaded.

Inspired by *The Book Thief* by Markus Zusak.

Epiphany

The rider praised the steadiness
and thriftiness of his *Burro*:
the safest, sanest riding mount
over many long years,
save when something spooked her
whereat she'd trip and pitch him forward
which is precisely what happened
to the actor in this poem.

The next thing the rider knows
he starts to recite litanies
not at *Burro*, no, no— but at the old
McClellan saddle,
hard as stone, hard-on-the-arse bargain hunt
the best choice at the dingy shop,
painstakingly paid upfront.

Presently, *Burro* takes the lead
walks Rider off the road,
closer to the meadow
where gallant wind and pampas grass
frolic and catcall each other.
Then, either Burro does not know
or the mule is on to something

but Rider follows her idly
straight to the middle of a brook.
By and by, the rider suspires,
captivated while unfurling
as with tidal oscillation
Brook swells
and swallows *Burro* and Rider complete.

In the somnolence of twilight,
into his peripheral view
shimmies a crystal torchlight of
translucent silver tulle.
Loud exhales tumble out
as he traces up to its source
and with profusions of pleasure,
points and says to the mule:

The moon, look, look,
the phenomenal moon!
His enthusiasm draws the attention
of the rotund lady lamp, fazed.
She smiles, instantly enraptured
like a mother summoned to take notice
and with eyes enlarged, delighted,
stares dazzled at the satiny earthlings,
flailing—a man, a mule—*echt** perfections!

echt German, "real, genuine, authentic."

Calamitous Portend

Harsh, Harsh and unforgiving
macabre and floundering—the storm*
holding swaddled baby snug, I peek
through the chink in the curtains
the storm quivers the garden path,
rain stampedes the flowers
the wind's whistle—how it rings—
a barbaric loud, singing goblet!

the baby, like a caged bird, warbles
releasing a piercing trill, angry!
wind-wielded the storm comes
emerald-ed and blinding wet
whipping the roof, torturing the fields
unbearable and malevolent

above the baby's scream
black branches buck each other.
Weak, flimsy, vulnerable, my hope
—no solace and no God to pray to
I slide Baby's head to my chest
but the sound of my racing heart
doesn't soothe. Turbulent like a whiplashed
ship out at sea, we two—a soul
better come to save us, or else...

the door rattles, and the ruthless wind
wiggles in—snuffs out the candle
the baby quiets, and I hear
the furniture move, crashing us.
I howl, pained, as Baby's flung
from my arms. I can't hear him, but I
see a green thing—the size of Baby—
glide out the door and
like a rag doll—a ferocious force
flings me to the far wall.
A wheezing alerts me of a
presence; I move to it—
There is a God. There is a God!

* Inspiration for this poem came from reading Ted
Hughes poem, 'Wind.'

Fissured

Fissured in a strange place
I drop to my knees and sit
still with my emotions

ashen light filters through
the charred branches to highlight
all the dangling pieces

I gather the shards, hold them to the light
as a dowry of my seething sadness
— the pieces rearrange and activate

my hurts ooze green nebulae
unhesitatingly turn to seeds—
I scatter them for the pigeons

with a prayer of rebirth
I watch the granivorous birds eat,
fly off into the distant blue.

The River

The river grumbles her complaint
to the smoke clouds that curl up
day in and day out from the factories

What on earth could they be making in there?

Disgust argues in her stomach,
even the mirror image in her waters lacks luster
now the green of the mountain was jet black

like soot on chimney walls— cumulonimbus that
never rain; clouds that keep outgrowing
into stiff peaks that lattice out the sun

blurring the indigo-blue edge of the mountains
gouging it from her sight
the clouds cloud the moon too

What on earth could they be burning?*

And who made them monads
that no eye could look into?
Oh, sad souls with not a stir of remorse!

the clouds darken,
the mountain rots
the river dries up.

*"What on earth could they be burning?" Words attributed to a poem titled 'Smoke' by Kenji Miyazawa. Page 65: Kenji Miyazawa. *Strong In The Rain—Selected Poems.* Translated by Roger Pulvers.

For an Hour

when a colorless day lets slip
a rare irreproachable hour

take it and indulge it for a while
sit with it, let it swallow you whole

or paint it with shades alluring,
dye each second with thoughts of hope

paint your steps from here to the seashore
pigment the waves to humor the sun

taint the sun—no, wait—don't paint the sun
we need Helios to stay as is

winnow the bulrush color-washed
clouds that camouflage Mt. Fuji

and the hawk—just let the hawk be
duly, a day will never beam

without bringing you a recall
of the sea, laughing with you for an hour

Kindred

A true story that I cherish
when December comes slip sliding
it's old-fashioned, humble, love-filled
and decidedly December.
So, grab a chair and draw in close
as I tell you about my childhood
in a land where stars are plenty
closets lack coats—hearts aren't empty!

It never snowed on Christmas Day
nor at any time of the year
so the job fell on Dad to forge
white Christmases year after year.
In the humble-est of efforts,
we saw him scratch his head and gloat
as he passed ideas by Mom
who'd nod and smile, making pig grunts.

The excitement from the town folks
brought buzz that sped up November
for the sundry store-tailor shop
to build a great show and bring snow.
On the first day of December
did appear a pure white Christmas
in the window of a store in
a small town in a small country.

Balls of cotton, elongated,
patted flat, garlanded the floor
wire hangers shaped as twinkly stars,
candy canes, snowflakes, and toy horns.
Mom's doilies from Good-Housekeeping
garnered praise and conversations
a plastic snowman 'tween snowflakes,
the jolly Santa, wee toy drums.

Trumpets, airplanes, ribbons and dolls,
broomstick horses, storybooks, sprites;
Victorian cards, fake holly,
painted pinecones—did folks dazzle!
Rocking robins, talismans, doves
little toy soldiers with toy guns.
And in the middle, the tallest
Christmas tree, ornaments and lights.

But in our cozy rooms—the rest of the house
the new linoleum and Christmas curtains
the present wrapping and more decorating,
the advent calendar and Christmas baking,
the greeting cards and hallmark apples,
the Santa letters and Christmas stockings,
the record player and joyful carols.
Poinsettias, doilies, kugels, Dresdens,
the nativity with the boy-child, and
the angel atop the table Yule tree—
joys that set our little hearts ablaze.

For the rest of my days,
when December comes slip sliding
humble love memories I trace — decidedly December.
Daddy brought us white Christmases
to revel and boast,
and Mommy brought us Yuletide joy to last forever.

Reproach

It's all about the angle
and weightage that you house
if you laze the hours often,
forever will outlive you

you'll dwell in dread, numb, empty
unrest will drag you down
to find that Summer lapsed by,
a long Winter ensuing

henceforth, when you seek the timeless
forever might seem short
an error of perception
you cannot reproach the stars

The Lore

Azure and unperturbed is the sky
until a little cloud perches high
above me near sunset
I quit my book
glad Cloud stopped for me.

We stare at each other long,
me, blanking out toils and troubles,
Cloud turning orange and peach until she
mauves herself, melding with Sky,
and follows it.

When I can discern her no more
I walk away from my tent—down
to the small river that gurgles.
I watch it gain speed, and as it
snakes into the noble Pacific

I hear her babble me a goodbye.

A salacious wind blows warm air
behind my ear but soon disowns me,
a moth brushes on my temple and
is gone much too soon.

Everyone's on the move except me—

I don't mind, I have the chant of the
river, the bustling of bugs,
puddles of moonlight, silhouetting
the beauteous forms of things
and best of all, and best of all
the seven daughters of Atlas
clustered over me.

What else do I need?

Sentencing

She polished her exterior well
wore her Sunday best—
smelled of mothballs.
No one dare convict her son
based on her appearance.

Someone ushered her to a seat—
in the middle, the third row.
She need not move her head
only her eyes from side to side
to grasp the scale of the situation.

The rim of her hat and her chest
point sharply at the judge
her eyes bounce from the jury to
her son, sometimes stopping
to pierce the back of this
woman's fat head
set decorously in the front row.

What good was that now?
What makes a woman that brazen?
To hold the whip,
demand he lopes
from one job to another,
nixing him repose on their bed—
Working cows don't sleep in beds,
insisting.

With stale-larded bread, she sends him off
and half a portion, at that,
of what she eats and serves their plump brats.
Oh! How she disliked that woman,
not fit for her son, who
heartlessly provoked his demise.

When her eyes meet the wild
wide eyes of her son,
emplaced with his lawyer—
strutting a timid little mustache
and as scrawny as him—
she sees her boy.
Her eyes fog, recalling
the many times she saw
the universe in those wild eyes.

Those eyes mesmerized her
with their neediness
and so she served him first—
half of whatever was in the pot
while she and the girls made do
with the other half.

You love him best, the girls argued
as they filed to their beds hungry...
Her shoulders deflate,
she slouches and rubs her wrists
as if feeling handcuffed. Soon
she catches her second wind.
That woman— she was his downfall
— they should put her in jail!
without explanation,
banning her from stopping home to
collect clean underwear.

I Forgot

Something in how she raised her chin
in greeting, and how her eyes
squinted told me
she was someone who knew me—
from grade school, perhaps,
or church choir? Someone.

Someone who smelled like my grandma's
kitchen on Sundays. Someone
I must have teamed with
to play marbles with the boys,
spent long hours with, and
talked to until dark.

Someone I shared secrets with— that
someone, a wind clued me.
But as she reached for my shoulder
I backslid, pretending to
suddenly recall
what I'd entered for.

I dodged her, withheld an ilk hello
like old times,
as old friends do. But.
I forgot my manners.
I forgot her name.
I even forgot why I was there.
I just forgot.

Soliloquy

Of the flock, the hues turn pale
from the same tree, apples expire
but strength is found in the numbers
last I checked, three is much higher.

Three are planning a reunion
the news reached me through the wire
of course, I was not invited
that would be no fun for the choir.

Who does she think she's fooling
flaunting more talent than the rest,
the same home that housed her, nursed us,
food slimmed her; us, fattened and stressed.

Not fighting the fight like Ma' taught
Surrendering, and winning, still
talking froth about dandelions
guarding smiles to bring out at will.

Inhaling sun from line-dried sheets,
collecting dust from neutron-stars,
seeing rainbows on pitch-dark nights
protecting fireflies in glass jars.

On and on, in torrents of fire,
fawning on their merits through mine,
waste a good night disparaging
with nothing but me on their minds.

Why wouldn't I be the anti
to balance the scales above all
a red pill, a blue pill—that's why
there's fewer of us after all.

But strength is found in the numbers
collectively, three's still higher,
of course, they would not invite me
I'd bring no fun in their hell's mire.

Lux of Human Wisdom

In my meager calculations, somewhere southeast of
that swift-moving cloud and the sound of waves
slapping, I lost something of great value.

And somewhere between there and the bleached moon
I found it but lost it again:

Paused at the door of the Universe's lost and found—
a stretch of words, of short hymns and mist trails
swerving skyward—I glanced around at feeble
present progressive faces like mine

And Universe, without cosmic remorse
continued on its constant course.
...
Southeast of a westerly gliding cloud, somewhere in
the sub-stratosphere, I come upon a puddle of water.
In its midst a blue hyacinth lays—I pick up the flower
of rain, inhale deeply its sweet licorice balsamic scent,
and, humbled, regard long my reflection in the puddle.

In a trice, my soul recalibrates me.
Through wet lashes, I see myself and flower:
I sneeze into a rainbow, and I *find* me!

Slice of Life

Flanked between two wanings, I *live* you,
planting the light hours with loving acts,
for you, for us, for our ménage,
and when I meet the dusk, filled,
ready for our mingling at the table,
where we swap slices of lived moments
of the same day, hearts swell replete.

Awe, Heart so Complete*

Awe, heart so wild and yet so peaceable
with changeable hues of blue and ashen
at times turns balmy under lilacs warmth
and at others, shimmers and then glistens
reflecting a streak of silver golden
that hatchets the surface, scythes it in two
offspring of mine, my vast aquatic babe,
from henceforth, I christen you 'Marina'

Awe, heart untamed yet imperturbable
to me, my dear, you are Mar-reen-awe
an imposing name that even falls short
of encompassing the awe that grips my heart–
for something as majestically wild,
mysterious, poised, and unbound as you
in each drop, you bear the tears of heartbreak
with sensuality, finesse, and warmth.

Awe: heart so serene, yet volatile—
reproach the moon and weather conditions
(or is it, maybe, the other way around?);
humankind approach to regard you: some
to empty their souls and learn to relent,
some to measure and weigh the strength of you;
to comprehend your charged powers, and charms
or arrive to dream of dreams yet to be
and ask you to whisper them out yonder.

Awe, heart so big, complete, and unafraid,
that holds secrets and promises, many—
never forgets; bequeaths remedies whole,
to calm the wild torrents of troubled souls
and sets spirits free to sail on renewed
I'll take you just as you are, Marina.
always, forever, Aquamarine Awe!

Dedicated to my Editor, Ingrid Wilson

Author Bio

Selma Martin is a retired English teacher with 20 years of teaching children ESL.

She believes in people's goodness and in finding balance in simple living. She lives in Japan with her husband.

In 2017, after retiring from her ESL position, Selma enrolled in her first short story writing competition with The Write Practice (TWP), a welcoming online community of writers. She practiced earnestly there and had the honor of mingling with seasoned Writers and newcomers like herself.

In 2018, Selma participated in a TWP networking course whose final lesson was to publish a story on Amazon. After many failed attempts, she completed the course, and self-published her short story, "Wanted: Husband/ Handyman," in 2019.

Later, collaborating with peers from that course, she published "Wanted: Husband/Handyman" in Once Upon A Story: A Short Fiction Anthology.

Selma has published articles and poems on Medium since 2017; she has the story from that first competition published in Short Fiction Break, 2017, and poetry in The Poetorium At Starlight, 2022, MasticadoresUSA, and Spillwords.

After her first NaPoWriMo 2021, Selma began to write poetry on her website, selmamartin.com, and struggled with her introversion to garner the courage to publish this—her first collection of poems.

You can find Selma, selmawrites, on Twitter, Instagram, and Facebook.

Kathryn A. LeRoy

Cover photographer Kathryn A. LeRoy creates stories with words and images to touch the heart of the world with kindness, courage, and wholeness. You can find Kathryn at kathrynleroy.com or catch her with her notebook and camera capturing moments of life.

Gratitude

The threads that embellish our lives are manifold and mixed. And we can only list them in hindsight. The thread about my writing is short, as it only started in 2017. And I see its length running ahead of me already. Let me unspool it for you.

Before this book existed, there was my Editor, Ingrid Wilson of EIF, who saw something in me when she agreed to help me polish my words well enough to send out into the world; a reality that I felt far-fetched. But before my Editor, there were others—some obvious, and some not: my blogging friends and supporters in the WordPress Reader Community; my faithful WordPress readers and newsletter pen pals; my website designer; my untiring Active Alumni tribe that let me run ideas and sometimes bloated first drafts for publication 'one day.' They were my best cheerleaders. Thank you.

Joe Bunting and his team of word enthusiasts at The Write Practice (TWP), Ruthanne Reid and Sarah Gribble—the best writing coaches and motivators; Podcasters—particularly Sarah Werner of Write Now Podcast through whose guidance I learn about social media and websites. She spotlighted me to Jeff, who then pointed me to The Write Practice. Thank you so much!

My bestie (whom I've never met in person but whose cursive handwriting I know so well).

She lives in Texas and was my extra set of eyes when I first wrote these poems. She is also the one behind the camera who graciously gifted me the photograph that became the cover of my book. Our book. A heart over-flowing with gratitude, Kathryn LeRoy. (see her Author bio).

And the same big heart with gratitude for my adult sons, who helped me learn how to operate the hand-me-down iPad on which I listened to podcasts. Also, a staircase was only a staircase until you two came into my life. After that, your dad and I became hawks. I love the humans you have become, and my heart knows no limits—for helping me change how I see the world. It's a much better place with you in it. I love you guys, and sharing this love with your special partners increases it. Thank you for bringing us so much music, laughter, and kindness.

Finally, to my dearest husband of thirty-three years, who completes me. Thank you for sharing this publishing journey with me and for being the best companion to me in this life. I'm so happy to be walking every day with you.

I dedicate this book to all my readers, who, from now on, are part of a new thread in my story. Thank you from the bottom of my heart.

Also Available from EIF

Re-Create & Celebrate
by Cindy Georgakas

ISBN: 9781739404413

In this unique book, Cindy guides her readers through simple steps to achieve the life they have always dreamed of. Not simply life goals, but a whole new outlook and way of living. Through her transformational techniques and practices, which she has gained from decades of experience in the field of life coaching, she provides a teaching memoir and workbook containing the tools to build a blueprint to a life of fulfillment, inner peace and happiness.

The Colourblind Grief
by Jude Gorini

ISBN: 9781739404406

London 2011, the year before the Olympics. The city is buzzing, and Daniel is just starting his journey into self-destruction: living a life of toxic love as his only remaining option. Sex, drugs and rock & roll are his sustenance. His mental health issues warp his life. 10 years later, everything has changed. Was it just a lie created by his family, or by his mind?

Archery in the UK
by Nick Reeves and Ingrid Wilson

ISBN: 9781739757786

Inspired by the *Lyrical Ballads* of Wordsworth and Coleridge, two authors set out to pen a contemporary homage to this timeless collection. As the collaboration progresses, however, the poetry and the unique narrative it carries takes on a life of its own. Thus, the authors come to tell their story through a collection of ballads, sonnets, pantoums and other forms.

40 Poems At 40
by Ingrid Wilson

ISBN: 9781739757700

40 Poems is the debut poetry collection from Ingrid Wilson. It is poetry of place and space, and here lie the clues and the beauty to Wilson's poetry. Her work is charted, landscaped, travelled, explorative and laden with adventure. There are bright, sad, dreamy postcards telling of the beauty of Barcelona, the slate-grey, but singing, county of Cumbria, Malaga, 'the emptiness' of Manchester, 'the fields' of London, 'the ancient pasts' of Newcastle, the mysterious beauty of Slovenia, Venice and its lullaby... lapping water is never far from her ear.

Wounds I Healed: The Poetry of Strong Women, edited by Gabriela Marie Milton

ISBN: 9781739757724

Award-winning authors, Pushcart nominees, emerging poets, voices of women and men, come to the fore in this stunning, powerful, and unique anthology. These poems testify both to the challenges that women face in our society, and to their power to overcome them. A memorable collection of over 200 poems by more than 100 authors, this anthology is a must-have for all lovers of poetry.

Nature Speaks of Love and Sorrow
by Jeff Flesch

ISBN: 9781739757755

In this hotly-anticipated debut poetry collection from Jeff Flesch, the author invites us to take a voyage with him through trauma and pain into acceptance and bliss in the embrace of nature itself. Jeff's poems are infused with the textures and colours of the natural world, and his journey through this sensory paradise provides the backdrop to his inner journey towards healing and growth.

Three-Penny Memories, A Poetic Memoir
by Barbara Harris Leonhard

ISBN: 9781739757762

"Do you love your mother?"

— This provocative question provides the catalyst for this stunning poetic memoir from Puschart Nominee Barbara Harris Leonhard. Through her artfully crafted poetry, the author considers where her love and loyalties lie following her aging mother's diagnosis with Alzheimer's.

Printed in the USA
CPSIA information can be obtained
at www.ICGtesting.com
LVHW021113191123
764350LV00033B/773